Profits from the sale of this book will go to Parkinson's UK

The Bonny Road
-Myths and Legends

By The Lichfield Poets

A Fishbowl Publishing Anthology

FBP05

Edited by Emily Rose Galvin

Cover Photo by Phil Binding

Published in association with

Fishbowl Publishing Limited

fishbowlpublishing.com

ISBN: 9781797405285

The Bonny Road
-Myths and Legends

A Lichfield Poets' Anthology

Thomas the Rhymer

'O do you see that narrow road,
So thick beset with thorns and briers?
That is the path of righteousness,
Though after it but few enquires.

'And do you see that broad, straight road,
That lies across the meadows' flowers?
That is the path of wickedness,
Not the way to heaven's bowers.

'And do you see that *bonny road*,
Which winds about the green hillside?
That is the road to fair Elf land,
Where you and I this night must ride.

About the extract from Thomas the Rhymer
These three verses are from a traditional ballad that was probably
composed in about 1700. The original language, characteristic of the
Scottish Borders, has been slightly adapted in this extract by Sarah Dale.
Thomas the Rhymer, also known as True Thomas, travelled to Elfland with
the Queen of the Fairies. When he came back he could see the future, but
was unable to lie.
Many people will have heard the version by Steel Eye Span, first recorded in
1974 on the album Now We Are Six.

Foreword

Parkinson's Disease is the second most common degenerative neurological condition after Alzheimer's. It affects 1 in 500 people and is caused by the death of nerve cells in the part of the brain called the Substantia Nigra. No one knows why, and there is no cure.

Quite simply it is awful. There is not an area of your body or life it does not affect for the worse and when you stagger, slur or struggle to put on your coat, people will laugh and call you drunk. I know, it has happened to me. Then there are the people who help. So, it is both a joy and an honour to write the foreword to 'The Bonny Road'. Who knows - it might provide the wherewithal for the cure?

I cannot thank The Lichfield Poets enough for giving their time and their talent in the production of this book and thank you for buying it. Don't stop there, read it. It is fantastic.

John Mills

Witchery Hole

Haggard, bent,
draped in rags, dragged
from her Birch Farm familiars.

Sentenced at Brooklyn
she should have drowned but
the Teme spat her out.

Stake bound, as if to cauterize a superstition,
her skin sears, blisters, bursts
spitting vituperative pus into

the purifying flames. Body, wood and ignorance
meld together in a sulphurous
denunciation of the flesh

which is buried, north south,
amongst the wreckage of her cats,
beneath the tartan charm of our picnic blanket.

John Mills

Introduction

Thank you for taking your first steps along 'The Bonny Road'!

The Lichfield Poets are a group of local writers. They meet every couple of weeks to chat about poetry, enjoy creative workshops or work on projects such as this book. They decided it was time to showcase the talents of the members and support a worthy charity along the way.

The idea for 'The Bonny Road' came from work done for a local spoken word project on Myths and Legends. Contributors were encouraged to think about traditional stories as well as to invent new urban myths. We decided that this would be a good theme for a book and set about gathering work from our members.

The idea to support Parkinson's UK came from our high regard for an associate of The Lichfield Poets who has Parkinson's. Despite this he is able to write and deliver his work at many spoken word events and maintains a good-humoured approach to his poetry, and to life in general.

This gave us the idea to use the subject of myths and legends as the basis for our book. There is much misinformation and misunderstanding of Parkinson's and how it affects people. It is a cruel disease which robs people of their mobility and can eventually leave them severely disabled. However, there is much evidence to suggest that remaining active and positive can slow down or mitigate the effects. Modern medication is developing all the time.

So please enjoy the creative fruits in this book. We hope you find the poems thought-provoking and uplifting. Proceeds from 'The Bonny Road' will go to Parkinson's UK and help them support people with the disease and the development of more effective treatments.

Thank you.

Phil Binding
The Lichfield Poets.

Monster or Myth?

They seek her here
by heather covered mountains,
under cold, dark waters.

They seek her there
in caves below
ancient ruined castle.

They seek her everywhere.
Cameras poised, waiting
to snap her, trap her.

Is she swan-necked
with one or more humps,
or only a movement of waves?

She's not a plesiosaur,
She's not a kelpie.
Still they come to Scotland

to find our Nessie.
But is she monster
or simply a fake tourist attraction?

Marjorie Neilson

Narcissus and the Broken Mirror

Narcissus watched in horror,
as his beloved mirror slipped
from his hands, and splintered
into a million different pieces.

His face, contorted in rictus sorrow,
reflected in ugly lines from the floor,
and the sharp ends of that which gave
him so much pleasure
now only causes him pain.

He longs to glue the mirror back together,
but the lines that he leaves
reflect the ugly reality,
rather than the face that he
and the rest of the world once loved.

For when something that gave you pleasure
is gone, it is better to find something new,
and not fix the same thing that now cuts
your hands every time you pick it up.

Ben Macnair

Narcissus

And now
A burden / a curse

My beauty an albatross
Worn in clipped rings and screaming-
This be me. Or be this me.

I am, the visual wealth of the richest man

I am the river. I am spring;
Sprung to life / objectifying

I am masturbation, multitudes of self-satisfaction
Gratification, if only I was cast to an eye-
Upon your echoing voice, as I spurn you away to be one with
the grass, turning worms with your curling toes.

For no one may win the heart of a man who owns his own.

Mother, marry me to the river
I met the man I wish to wed,
To bed,
Lay down thy bow, the hunt is over
To bed
Rest
To bed.

Caught eyes drown in time and tide.

Phillip Knight

Waiting for You

They called him Icarus behind his back.
He worshipped strange Gods,
sometimes flew way too high
on clouds of fantastic fallacy.
Gazing through lonely spectacles
he named his deities and desires.
The TV was imperious Zeus,
all-knowing, all seeing, almighty.

His car, madly motoring Mercury;
laptop computer - gentle Athena
stroking his awkward obsessions.
Helios lit his bedtime lamp
casting underworld shadows
across the Styx of his bathtimes!
Medusa lived in a writhing tree,
shone fleece-golden in Olympian sunsets.

But his true love was mighty Hera,
Queen of Gods, deep urgent voice
cajoling in the deep rumble of
his churning, steaming dishwasher.
Besotted by midnight economy cycles,
Icarus spun with mounting devotion.
He spoiled her with fresh salt
and the finest cleansing tablets.

He put his affairs in order, made ready,
crept to open the machine's door.
"I've been waiting for you," she said.
It was a while before he was missed.
The police report was routine;
missing person, no sign of foul play,
smeared spectacles on the kitchen floor.
Forensic tests said "rinse aid."

Phil Binding

<u>Luthien's Lament</u>

Our love
Is the radiance clutched in severed hand
The brilliance of light
Carved from the innards of beasts
That no darkness could pry from the meeting of our
forbidden eyes

Our love
Is the twilight song of a nightingale
Each note that twirls through the canopy of moonlight
Royal feet sparkling their naked path through a dancehall of
beech and fern

Our love
Is equal parts
A silent footprint left upon moss
The dripping maw and bared teeth of wolves
The hollow wind of loss that whips through white sails borne
for eternity

Our love
Is measured within each other
And as my voice tears through the halls of my Elders
To me this grandeur,
This haven, means nothing
I give all to you
My eternity for your numbered days
I give my life to meet you
Across a gulf you may never sail

Our love
Would be a wish granted
To dance again with nightingales
And rest together in the cradling arms
Of mountains cast in blue.

Emily Rose Galvin

The Myth of Snowflakes

So much unused magic lives in silence,
when we hear the quiet clash of icebergs,
temporary, monstrous, melting,
and gone, before their existence goes unnoticed.

Ben Macnair

A Thousand Origami Cranes

Origami cranes flew from her fingers
in every shade of paper;
a thousand is the magic number
for a wish
and she wished you well.

The house was full of cranes
roosting on every surface,
shelves, picture frames,
tins in the larder –
each a folded hope.

Maybe she made too many or too few;
the magic did not work;
she went about her life,
slightly damaged
like all the girls who love you.

Years later the occasional crane
still emerges from some hidden place,
a little bent and dusty
but long neck still stretched
raised wings ready for flight.

Cranes are good house guests;
they don't make a noise –
the only mess is when
they flutter to the floor
and cannot rise.

We also fail to fly;
stubborn as rats in a maze
we tread our path,
knowing there is no exit
yet hoping we may find it.

This is a kind of courage,
not blazing or heroic
all crash and fire and shouting,
but constant endurance,
a search for some grace.

Longing to hear beating wings,
to look up and see cranes flying,
feel the strong, sure beat of wings;
hear music of cranes calling
as they fly overhead.

Sarah Dale

Bells Call

An imaginary translation from the Kanji

Whenever bells call, Grandfather sits,
shoulder muscles strained, radiating tension,
waits for their pealing's end.
No-one knows his misery's root,
we have always been mystified.
To all enquiries, he shrugs,
speaks slowly, as to children
"It is beyond your understanding."

Gary Carr

River Spirit

It must be a wild night thick with thunder,
inquisitive gusts probing harassed hair,
waves banging banks like battering rams,
sudden swings of breaking branch.

On this night of clapped cloud,
momentary moonshine and moaning
tree, you may glimpse the Goddess,
splitting surface and scattering swan.

She rides the water's rough ridges,
cries calamity and chaos to fools,
strikes fire and fear to bed and bough
urges the unsleeping to take heart.

If you are lucky she may spot you
slinking under silver birch and beech,
pierce you softly with her sweet sword.
You will be bountifully blessed!

As your river descends from spring
through twist and merry meander
easing to submission in your final sea,
say a prayer for the River Spirit.

She will be waiting for you there.

Phil Binding

The Man Who Didn't Lay the Table

I heard from a friend of a friend,
Of a man who lived at the end
Of the street of the town of Stace,
Who said he would not set a place.

At night the elves gathered to meet,
To meet and greet and eat and eat
But they could only stand and stare
At the table not laid, but bare.

On New Year's Eve tables are set
For House Elves food and drink is left
"N-N-N-No food", they stuttered.
"This is outrageous", they muttered.

What do we do? What do we say?
How do we teach him to behave?
Do we hit him, kick him, shove him?
Do we laugh at him, shout at him?

Do we smash the house, trash the house?
Do we turn him into a mouse?
We will do nowt, we will get out
A sly Gremlin, will then come in.

In deepest winter, man and elf
Renew their pact, the light to keep,
But where the pact is broken
In, the dark, will creep...

Ian Ward

The Iceman Cometh

He dances in the night
Weaving webs of dazzling gossamer.
Leaping over continents-
A pirouetting force of energy
Spinning and spirited,
Lightest tiptoe of acrobatic dance.
Releasing magic crystals of ice
That gently coat the land in white.
"Ha ha!" he laughs twirling faster,
Ever restless, never still.

A chime of tiny bells chinkle and ting.
"A touch of rimed mist here.
A shake of diamonds there!"
He spreads beauty in his passage,
Leaving tracery on glass,
Mirrors on water.
An avalanche of sapphires and citrine,
The world glinting in rainbow light.
Tiny snowflakes dust his lashes,
His eyes radiant aquamarine.

He feels slight warmth on his back
Leaps vast surging oceans,
Summits peaks and pinnacles
Showering down renewed gems
Which glint and radiate in frozen hue.
Bounding back to his kingdom,
His icy retreat.
His throne carved from glacier ice
Where blizzards whip and whirl,
To aid his sleep. Give sweet rest.

"Ha ha! I'll be back!" he laughs.
"With more rare treats",
His tinkling timorous voice
Ricocheting on the breeze!

Sue Wood

The Legend of the Tooth Fairy

Children place their teeth under pillows
and fall asleep, the Tooth Fairy enters
unseen, unheard, undisturbed and exchanges
the denticles for coins. It was always so.

No, it wasn't. Once upon a time a lost tooth was planted
in a garden or field hoping a permanent one would grow
and a witch wouldn't know where to find it and put a curse
on the child. But sometimes fires were the only safe places
to throw them and protect children from tooth discovery and
doom.

Dirt and fire were replaced by flower pots, planter boxes
and later
pillows, slippers,
necklaces, glasses of water,
beds (under)
roofs (over)
trees (inside)

Retrieval by
fairies, mice, lizards.
Squirrels, beavers, pigs.

Different traditions for different countries,
all offering: magic, gifts for children,
the joy of showing off their gummy gaps,
and creating stories of what the fairy does with their teeth:

Uses them for money in tooth fairy land.
Gives them to elves and gnomes to turn into fairy gems.
Plants them in the garden and grows children.
Turns them into seashells for fish to live in.
Makes sparkling clothes out of them.
Grinds them into fairy dust and sprinkles it on herself;
that's the magic that makes her fly.

Janet Jenkins

Three Haiku on Trees

1.
Oak tree unbending
may fall in a fearsome wind:
Sway like the marsh reed.

2.
Tree that bears no fruit
Should not be destroyed in haste:
It may store honey.

3.
The willow tree weeps
Into the rushing water:
Angler waits for catch.

1. based on Aesop's fable No. 92
The Oak and Reed.

2. based on Aesop's fable No. 86
The Peasant and the Apple Tree

3. based on prompt at Samuel Johnson's House
On the theme of 'Willow' for National Writing Day.

Marjorie Neilson

A Weeping Willow Legend

Once we grew upright,
until our ancestors saw
two young lovers die.

They drooped in sadness
and have never recovered;
we have to mourn too.

Janet Jenkins

An Updated View

I'd like to be a cheerful tree,
but how can I when my name
denotes sadness?
My beautiful branches hang down
conveying the falling of tears;
how I'd like them to be tears of laughter.

My family are remembered for death
and mourning, magic, omens and ghosts
and it's said we can have power over
the moon, water and even other willows.

I have power over nothing; I stay
here day after day minding my own
business, bending and blending with nature.
Admire me if you wish, then come and talk
to me; raise my spirits, if not my branches.

Janet Jenkins

The Gilbertstone – Blakesley Hall

Hewn from the tallest cliff
The craggiest crag
The roughest rock
It stands defiant as a dragon's tooth
Wrenched from unyielding ancient strata
To claim ancient lands
When monsters roamed, wolves marauded
And bears lay in wait
Yet this was Gilbert's land
With the strength of a hundred oxen
And the determination of a thousand men
He dropped his rock, marker
Sign of his great giant's power
Left to leave lesser giants in fear
And mere mortals in awe
Bulging menacingly from the ground below
As some would have it, Giant Gilbert's Toe.

Gary Longden

Spilt Milk

You are a spilt river of milk, washing me away

Toad, dear toad
give me one wish, one small wish,
and I'll give you milk –
warm and sweet in a silver dish,
smooth as silk
You are grapes withered on the vine -
if tears were wine
we'd raise a toast to grief

Toad, dear toad
grant me a wish, one little wish,
and I'll sew you a gown –
velvet and lace, fine as the queen's
in London town
If tears were rain
the flooded world would drown -
washing us away

Toad, dear toad,
only one wish, one tiny wish,
and I'll make your bed –
fine satin sheets and goose feather pillows
to lay your head
You are the salted field that will not bear -
if tears were stars
night would outshine bright midday

Toad, dear toad,
give me a wish, one little wish,
and I'll give you my knife –
good sharp steel in a leather case
to take my life
If tears were blood
rivers would run rust red -
washing us away

"What is human life or grief to me?
Perfect in my skin and in my place
my magic is my own.
Broken stays broken;
nor tears nor sighs can fix it."

You are a spilt river of milk, washing me away

Sarah Dale

Railway Bridge, Lichfield

Rounding the corner from the City Station
You meet the 19thC railway bridge
Nondescript, it links a redbrick
Wall and the chip-shop opposite.

Ashlar abutments support plain plinths
Upon which four bluff shields
Hunker between the rivets and
The iron plates

Then the eye snags upon one queer shield
Squatting in the murk
The scene imprinted looks plain weird:
Medieval, as though

History's narrative had got jumbled up
Picked out in simple bas-relief
Figures lounge upon the ground
Clad in antique garb, they've lost their

Limbs in a fit of absent-mindedness
De-coupled arms and legs
Sprawl at large
In a state of casual neglect.

Something bad has been going on;
Photoshopped into the bridge arch
Where the pigeons coo and crap
As the trains roll and rumble overhead,

Lurks this humdrum Killing Field
Where the slouching Dead
Implore the bustling passerby:
"Here witness poor Christians

Snuffed out by our Roman occupiers.
The body is a fragile house", they say,
"Its limbs can snap and fray
And lie disorderly about

The vital force may leak away"
The English it seems worship defeat:
This blunt dismembering
Our rite of remembering

The bridge spans Roads and History
The shield a casting of the City's Etymology
Salve magna parens, Lichfield
It is said: the field of the dead

Phil Jones

Long Meg

I took a trip down the Eden Valley
to see Long Meg and her sisters.
They danced in a fell-shadowed glade,
whispering together so slowly
I could not hear their stony words.

Leaning gently in ancient earth
seemingly blind to a tilted zodiac,
piercing bewitched horizons
Long Meg watched over all
as laughing Eden bubbled by.

Cross Fell loomed in godlike gales,
spoke in hard winds, water-fat cloud.
I sat long in sad anticipation
as they moved to a parallel pace
in rocky dreams of transgression.

To them, eons rattle past
in brief flickers of day and night.
Seasons circle as minutes,
centuries career in hurried hours.
I was a blurred ghost, here and gone.

Phil Binding

Canterbury Journey

Perhaps such tales only end in trauma
Journeys thick with scalding oils
Painting drips and reformed faces.
And perhaps the Wife of Bath will forever wait upon the
Canterbury trail
With freedom of speech, freedom of being, freedom to lay
freely with untangled ankles for courtly love
Perhaps just looking for El Dorado itself
The four thousand mile meandering tentacle of promise to
seek ones own reward, ones own fame and fortune
In golden globes fighting forest like fingernails, clapping and
grabbing at insanity.
Ball gown paths, walking upon the lips of conceited strangers
Empty hollow gestures and reconstructed wreaths

The medieval are dead, dear boy

Or lost.
Between the divides of unknown
The folds of history
A solo flight, a solo woman, in charge of her own destiny, to
disappear

Or a right to choose
Not questioned
For what more can someone want
Than the freedom to not have to say

Yet we spoke upon our pilgrimage of words
Walking letters like wires and giggling down high speed rail -
once home to sacred lands
In treasured speak, across the cracked plates of continents
only to end where we began,

That no one really had an option, did they.

Phillip Knight

Mermaid at Birmingham University

No matter how much rain,
pavements oil slick with it,
fat puddles dimpling, gutters rilling,
no matter how much rain,
she is trapped by her tail.

No matter how wet the grass,
each long blade pearl weighted,
each meadow sweet umbrella
heavy with unshed water,
she needs more depth to swim.

She remembers the sea
as a phrase of broken music
heard through a closed window,
pane running with rain; still
she cannot cry a river.

Surfaces smooth and easy
for human feet defeat her;
stairs, bridges, roads, slopes
studded with shattered glass,
barbed wire embedded.

Someone should save her
from this desert – anyone
with a kind heart and strong arms,
to carry her to the canal –
let her slip in, go free, go home.

Sarah Dale

Grave Disorder

It is said that grave robbery is best done
under a full moon,
where only lunatics,
the drunk or the mad
might see you,
and their claims are easy to dismiss.

Take your best and sharpest spade,
and disturb the land that the grave-diggers just laid.
Have no concern for your morals,
respect for the recently deceased,
their family or their friends,
for what you might become.

Have no concern for your future,
your happiness, or your past.
Dig deep, and dig well,
for what is the human body,
but a temporary shell?

The dead are easily disturbed,
of that have no doubt,
but so will you be,
if you see the dead moving
at your own hand,
and you make deals
that you don't understand.

Graveyards under a full moon
are not safe places to thrive,
if you would to be sure to be make it out,
with your soul intact,
and the need to survive.

Ben Macnair

Woman Revisiting an Asylum

Roughly based on an anecdote from the British Museum's
Listening Project

In another lifetime
At seventeen, I was
Flytipped into a psychiatric
Home-
They were called asylums
In those days-

Looking at that person now
Is like seeing
Someone from afar
Who
Seems familiar but will not
Come into view.

I remember smells of
Cabbage, sudden
Muffled cries, nurses in white
Uniforms
Rules rigid as pokers
A sense of something withheld.

Many years later, 'cured'
I came back to
Photo-document the
Place
It seemed derelict, the
Past switched off.

The old ballroom where
Girls and boys stood numb
In two skewed lines, as though
Facing
A nervous firing squad
Was now derelict.

In the echoing room the
Mustiness stood tall
The floor bare, except one
Corner
Where the parquet
Floor seemed stained

By a litter of small paper scraps
On a closer view I saw it
Was a line of dead white
Butterflies
Their wings flat, like tiny sails
Dead souls, messengers

from another place.

Phil Jones

Holiday in Hell

All is silent, save for the drip of tears,
From the Ferryman's pole crossing the Styx,
There is a pause to tip the Ferryman.

Across limbo, all shades, but no shadow,
'Abandon hopes all ye who enter here.'
Hell's gate, Sin, Satan's mistress as keeper,
She holds the key, all may come, most may leave.

Demons sell special edition *Hello* magazine,
Hell's top hundred famous celebrities,
See and be seen with all the infamous.

Where it all began, selfie with that apple.
Preserved in Aspic, teeth marks highlighted,
A fruity whiff of forbidden knowledge
(Discount rate for those named Adam or Eve).

Stay at Angel's Rock, cheap though cheerless cliff,
The place to brood on the state of your soul.

Dining recommended by Weight Watchers,
Chez Tantalus - fine food, not quite in reach.

Piece-de-resistance of the visit,
Satan frozen at Hell's core, his three heads,
Weeping frustration, gnawing on sinners.
Please read the notice before entering;
'Warning, sinners may be at greater risk.'

Ian Ward

Lucifer – The Genius of Evil

Le génie du mal
Stoney wings surround his form.
Solid, chill, inflexible-
Offering a cloak of pale white marble
To disguise transgression.

Evil courses through
Each striation of the sculptor's tool,
Heft and hewn from ground stone.
So despicable his crime.
He sits within Cathedral niche-
Vulture-like, entombed.

Yet his beauty, his goodness was absolute.
The purest, the most beloved,
The most spectacular-
In seductive prime:
Morning Star, son of Dawn,
Fallen to the realms of the Dead.

In life, his pinioned feathers adorned with gems-
Soft burnished, bloodless white.
Topaz, sapphires, onyx, diamonds,
Crafted in lustrous gold.
The Archangel resplendent
In seducing insolence.

Membrane of wings veined and clawed.
His sculpted curls revealing devil's horns,
Broken Sceptre and crown in hand.
At his chained exquisite feet, the Apple of Despair.
In Beauty, divinity. In Evil, sublimity.
In Darkness, Inferno. In Light, Salvation.

Sue Wood

The Dragon Cote

Left on the platform, a pet carrier.
A pet carrier with smoke curling.
A crowded, busy train station platform.
Seemingly abandoned, in splendid isolation
Everyone swerving, stepping, walking around or over.
Through the twitch of legs, the smoke cleared, a label
appeared.
A voice came to me, not heard but felt,
Not felt but sensed, a tickle, a sniffle, a wiffle,
Words in my mind, thoughts in my brain
"Take me home, take me home" said the carrier.
I walked and the crowd parted without noticing.
It was a large, wicker-basket carrier,
A sturdy wicker handle with a grey tag
Platform 7a New Street Station
Another waft of smoke obscured the front.
Another thought and I take the escalator
With the carrier to a café in the Palisades.
Finally, basket on table, me on chair
I get to see its occupant
All I see is red, with a large snout and big, soft, brown eyes.
I opened the door and it slithered out
Fat, red body, four clawed feet,
Long, pointed tail, jointed, scaled wings
A baby dragon I say,
A house dragon I think.
This was how I met Wendle
My psychic, telepathic, psychedelic house dragon,
As close to a dragon as a cat to a tiger
A gentle creature who toasts bread rather than maidens.
No one believes in house dragons but me
With a psychic nudge people see what they want to see.
In the garden people see a dove cote
Not the dragon cote
Though they think the dove, a little scorched.

Ian Ward

When I Was a Building

For half a life you shared
your health, decisions,
victories and disappointments,
and an occasional summer cold
with me. In return I gave you
my plumbing and warmth,
my landscaping and red brick
intensity. Occasionally part of me
might die, one of you grow
a small outbuilding,
develop rust, require
preventative welding.

Now you have withdrawn,
packed, in front of me,
driven away to a younger place,
more tactile, electronically more
interactive.
I will pine, pare back
in half a century
to bare foundations,
and you...
you will never reach out
and open another window
at work
again.

Gary Carr

George Michael - Fallen Idol

Stage lights mesmerised him
like a flickering candle flame.

Music, the gift that brought him fame.
Words on staves betrayed his belief

that you should listen to your heart.
Yet, in life he found only grief.

His Achilles heel; vulnerability
afraid of whispers carelessly made.

So he hid behind false masculinity,
dark glasses and leather jacket.

The t-shirt said 'Choose Life'
but it became a poison chalice

filled with despair of the darkest colour
drowning him hour by hour,

one Christmas Day when all alone
his god visited; and called him home.

Marjorie Neilson

The Tutankhamen of Generation X

The room they found her in
was named, in gold-leaf,
on its walled-over door;
preserved beneath her
edge-sealed, woven nylon cover,
pen-stencilled "JOYCE".

Lifted out, uncovered,
beige curves blue-limned
in the flat faced glow
of her widescreen descendants,
she felt a dry-ribbon thirst,
four decades dreaming of ink.

And her hunger was for paper,
envelopes, a tri-part memorandum
lubricated with carbon paper,
to feed her golf-balled throat.
Her need was to rattle and shout
someone's words into a noisy office;

she wanted to communicate,
but her children had shrunk,
mutated. Spoke silently
as they called to the world
about this ancestor so far removed
that her DNA lived in every app.

Gary Carr

Cannock Chase. Who goes there?

Cannock Chase. Rolling hills, purple heather,
unspoilt miles of quiet tracks.
the perfect place for relaxation.

BUT troubled souls wander there, unable to rest;
a long-standing children's chant echoes these thoughts:

"When night falls, enter the woods at your peril,
"For inside lurks something worse than the devil.
"Avoid at all costs the gathering place,
"Where at midnight the pig-man roams on Cannock Chase."

Seven feet tall and dressed like a man,
from the neck down,
with a massive head and a snout-like nose.
squealing,
a loud high-pitched sound.

The Black- eyed child has been seen walking
through undergrowth trying to hide
her charcoal sockets, ,
no iris, no white, nothing.
The Lady of the Chase has appeared in headlights;
pale grey and naked with hypnotic eyes,
she left a couple too terrified to drive through the
woods again.

The tree-tall Slender Man, has floated and stretched
his limbs and body like warm toffee at least four times,
Related specters throughout the world induce the same fear.

And take note, panthers, wolves and Big Foot
could be lurking in the woods at any time
with UFO's hovering overhead and aliens ready to land.

Janet Jenkins

Journeys End

His journey complete,
He rests his feet on the grate,
Slips off soft shoes,
Rubs aching limbs.
The night has been long.
Satisfied he has given of his best,
Hoping his gifts will bring change,
He sips a small warming drink
Savours its sweetness,
Rubs his chin and thinks.

        "My, how things have changed", he reflects.

He knows inside, his gifts cannot bring
The transformation he desires…
All will be a momentary distraction
That cannot replace affliction, strain, grief.
He wishes his gifts could bring tranquillity, hope, peace…

        "No", he muses, and must brush such thoughts away.

My journey is over tonight.

I saw the Lodestar, the dawn break.
The burnished iridescence of ocean sheen.
Saw the world all clean, fresh, bright, pristine.
I am blessed…

Sue Wood

The Lichfield Poets

The Lichfield Poets was formed in 2007

It is a group for people aged 18 and over who have an interest in various aspects of poetry: reading, writing or performance. Activities include workshops and discussing poetry by group members and established poets.

Since its formation, members have previously produced two group charity books – 'Silver Words' for St Giles' Hospice and 'Battle Lines' for The National Memorial Arboretum-pamphlets on National Poetry Day poems, and one on *Imprisonment* which is in The Guild Hall gaol. Individual members have poems in The Samuel Johnson Birthplace Museum.

They have performed their own poetry at a number of events in Lichfield: the main festival, Literature, Jazz and Blues Festivals, and The Lichfield Mysteries, in addition to the Wolverhampton Literature Festival, Stafford Arts Festival and There is No Planet B events.

They have an Open Mic night called *Poetry Alight* every 2 or 3 months in The Brewhouse & Kitchen, Lichfield.

If you are interested in becoming a member, please contact - Lichfield.Poets@hotmail.co.uk

Fishbowl Publishing Limited

website - fishbowlpublishing.com

email – fishbowl.publishing@outlook.com

titles from fishbowl
available now and coming soon

(fbp01)   Anna *by* Emily Rose Galvin

(fbp02)   Midnight Messages *by* Phillip Knight

(fbp03)   Grace *by* Rebecca Lockwood

(fbp04)   Cockatiels and Bold Women

Printed in Great Britain
by Amazon